ALL AROUND THE WORLD
SOUTH KOREA

by Joanne Mattern

pogo

Ideas for Parents and Teachers

Pogo Books let children practice reading informational text while introducing them to nonfiction features such as headings, labels, sidebars, maps, and diagrams, as well as a table of contents, glossary, and index.

Carefully leveled text with a strong photo match offers early fluent readers the support they need to succeed.

Before Reading

- "Walk" through the book and point out the various nonfiction features. Ask the student what purpose each feature serves.
- Look at the glossary together. Read and discuss the words.

Read the Book

- Have the child read the book independently.
- Invite him or her to list questions that arise from reading.

After Reading

- Discuss the child's questions. Talk about how he or she might find answers to those questions.
- Prompt the child to think more. Ask: K-Pop is the name for popular music from South Korea. How does social media help spread music around the world?

Pogo Books are published by Jump!
5357 Penn Avenue South
Minneapolis, MN 55419
www.jumplibrary.com

Copyright © 2019 Jump!
International copyright reserved in all countries. No part of this book may be reproduced in any form without written permission from the publisher.

Library of Congress Cataloging-in-Publication Data

Names: Mattern, Joanne, 1963-
Title: South Korea / by Joanne Mattern.
Description: Minneapolis, MN : Jump!, Inc., 2018.
Series: All around the world | "Pogo Books."
Includes bibliographical references and index.
Identifiers: LCCN 2018000248 (print)
LCCN 2017061530 (ebook)
ISBN 9781624969270 (ebook)
ISBN 9781624969256 (hardcover : alk. paper)
ISBN 9781624969263 (pbk.)
Subjects: LCSH: Korea (South) –Juvenile literature.
Korea (South) – Description and travel–Juvenile literature.
Classification: LCC DS902 (print)
LCC DS902 .M33 2019 (ebook) | DDC 951.95–dc23
LC record available at https://lccn.loc.gov/2018000248

Editor: Kristine Spanier
Book Designer: Leah Sanders

Photo Credits: Nattee Chalermtiragool/Shutterstock, cover; tawatchaiprakobkit/iStock, 1; Pixfiction/Shutterstock, 3; gowithstick/Shutterstock, 4; Pius Lee/Shutterstock, 5; CJ Nattanai/Shutterstock, 6-7; Joshua Davenport/Alamy, 8-9; Guitar photographer/Shutterstock, 10; National Geographic Creative/Alamy, 11; Banditta Art/Shutterstock, 12 (top left); konmesa/Shutterstock, 12 (top right); Rudmer Zwerver/Shutterstock, 12 (bottom left); Wang LiQiang/Shutterstock, 12 (bottom right); Vitalii Hulai/Shutterstock, 14; Woojin Kim/123rf, 14-15; Photononstop/SuperStock, 16; Sean Pavone/Shutterstock, 17; bbtreesubmission/123rf, 18-19; 4kodiak/iStock, 20-21; Anurak Pongpatimet/Shutterstock, 23.

Printed in the United States of America at Corporate Graphics in North Mankato, Minnesota.

TABLE OF CONTENTS

CHAPTER 1

WELCOME TO SOUTH KOREA!

Visit an ancient **palace**. Walk along a **fortress** wall. Eat spicy cabbage. Let's take a trip to South Korea!

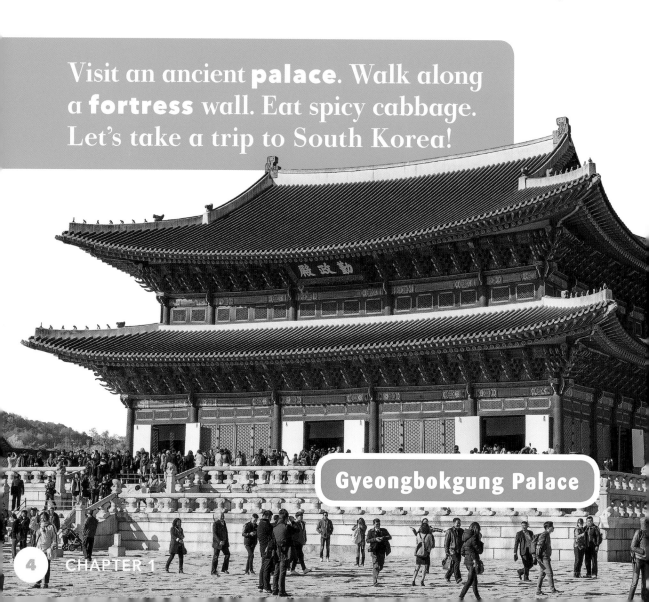

Gyeongbokgung Palace

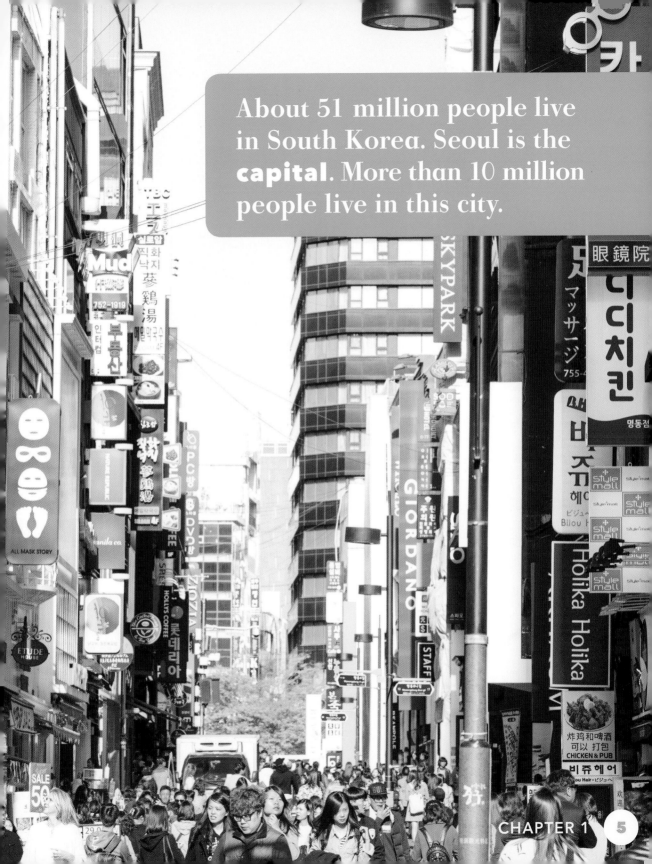

About 51 million people live in South Korea. Seoul is the **capital**. More than 10 million people live in this city.

South Korea's palaces were built more than 600 years ago. Royal families lived in them. Now they are museums.

Fortress walls built more than 200 years ago still stand. Visitors walk along the walls.

WHAT DO YOU THINK?

The fortress walls were built long ago to keep the area safe from **invaders**. What are some of the ways we stay safe now?

National Assembly Building

North Korea and South Korea were once one country. Ongoing disputes divided them in 1945. The two countries fought the Korean War between 1950 and 1953. These countries are still in conflict with one another.

South Korea is now a **presidential republic**. The government meets in the National Assembly Building. It is in Seoul.

DID YOU KNOW?

South Korea's flag is white. A blue and red symbol is in the middle. Black bars are around the sides. The flag symbolizes **balance**.

CHAPTER 2

CLIMATE AND CREATURES

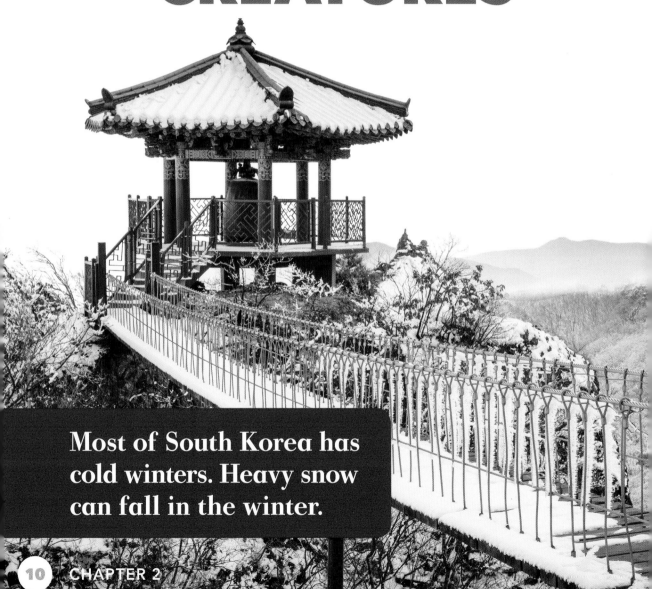

Most of South Korea has cold winters. Heavy snow can fall in the winter.

Summers are hot. **Typhoons** hit some parts of the country. These powerful storms bring wind and rain.

kingfisher

black bear

lynx

white-naped crane

The border between South and North Korea is called the DMZ. No people live here. It is now one of the most undeveloped areas in Asia. It is a **sanctuary** for hundreds of bird species. Black bears and lynx live here, too.

WHAT DO YOU THINK?

DMZ stands for "demilitarized zone." It has been untouched since the war. Why do you think animals stay safe here?

The Upo Wetland is in South Korea. Dinosaurs lived in the area 100 million years ago. Now more than 1,000 species live in the water. Water scorpions are here. So are fighting fish. Beautiful birds like swans, bean geese, and teals spend their winters here.

water scorpion

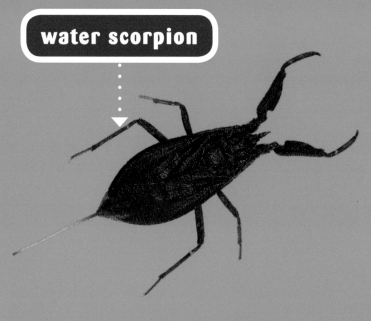

CHAPTER 3

LIFE IN SOUTH KOREA

Some people in South Korea are farmers. The main **crop** is rice. Fishing is an important job, too.

rice paddy

Most people here live in cities. They live in tall apartment buildings. City streets are crowded with people. Motorcycles and scooters zoom past. Many people work in factories. Others work in stores.

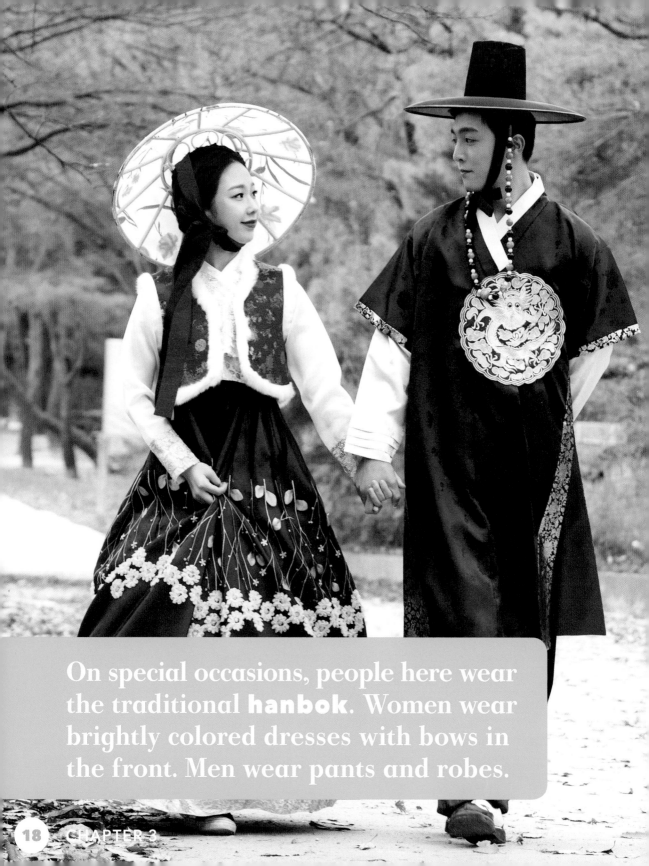

On special occasions, people here wear the traditional **hanbok**. Women wear brightly colored dresses with bows in the front. Men wear pants and robes.

TAKE A LOOK!

Wearing the hanbok more often is popular now. Why? People like posting pictures of it on **social media**. The traditional hanbok has many pieces to it.

DONGJEONG

OTGOREUM

JEOGORI

BAERAE

CHIMA

GAT

DURUMAGI

BAJI

KKOTSIN

Family and friends love to eat together. Kimchi is a favorite Korean food. It is spicy pickled cabbage. South Koreans also eat a lot of rice. They put barbecued beef and vegetables on top. This dish is called bulgogi. Rice cakes are a favorite snack.

South Korea is a beautiful nation! Would you like to experience its **culture**?

kimchi

bulgogi

QUICK FACTS & TOOLS

SOUTH KOREA

Location: Eastern Asia

Size: 38,502 square miles
(99,720 square kilometers)

Population: 51,181,299
(July 2017 estimate)

Capital: Seoul

Type of Government:
presidential republic

Language: Korean

Exports: computers, electronics,
cars and car parts, steel

balance: A condition in which opposing forces are equal to each other.

capital: A city where government leaders meet.

crop: A plant grown for food.

culture: The ideas, customs, traditions, and ways of life of a group of people.

fortress: A place that is fortified against attack.

hanbok: Traditional Korean clothing characterized by vibrant colors and simple lines.

invaders: People who enter an area for conquest or plunder.

palace: A large, fancy home for a ruler.

presidential republic: A system of government in which the president is the leader and has significant powers.

sanctuary: A natural area where birds or animals are protected.

social media: Websites and apps that help people connect with one another.

typhoons: Violent tropical storms.

INDEX

TO LEARN MORE

Learning more is as easy as 1, 2, 3.

1) Go to www.factsurfer.com

2) Enter "SouthKorea" into the search box.

3) Click the "Surf" button to see a list of websites.

With factsurfer, finding more information is just a click away.